Tinisha Thank

HIS MASTERPIECE:
A Royal Journey Of Self Discovery In God

A Memoir by Kendra Diggs
Foreword by Pastor Otis Lockett Jr

Support

Leadership Develop ME, LLC

You are His Masterpiece
Kendra

Copyright © 2019 Kendra Diggs

Book Package and Publication:
Leadership DevelopME, LLC: www.leadershipdevelopme.com

CREDITS

Book Cover Design:
Nicole Hubbard of Higher Touch Design Studio

Photography:
Luguzy Atkins of LA Photography

Headpiece: Demetra Oliver

First Draft of Book: Charisse Beverly

All rights reserved. No part of this book may be used or reproduced by any means, graphic, electronic, or mechanical, including photocopying, recording, taping or by any information storage retrieval system without the written permission of the publisher except in the case of brief quotations embodied
In critical articles and reviews.

Books may be ordered through booksellers or by contacting:

Kendra Diggs
Website: www.thekweenexperience.com

Because of the dynamic nature of the Internet, any web addresses or links contained in this book may have changed since publication and may no longer be valid. The views expressed in this work are solely those of the author and do not necessarily reflect the views of the publisher, and the publisher hereby disclaims
any responsibility for them.

Any people depicted in stock imagery provided by Thinkstock are models, and such images are being used for illustrative purposes only.

Certain stock imagery © Thinkstock.

ISBN: 978-0-359-53285-8
Library of Congress Control Number: 2019937648

Scripture quotations are taken from the Holy Bible, New Living Translation, copyright ©1996, 2004, 2015 by Tyndale House Foundation. Used by permission of Tyndale House Publishers, Inc., Carol Stream, Illinois 60188.

Printed in the United States of America

All rights reserved worldwide.

DISCLAIMER: This is based on a true story, a memoir, certain names and places have been changed in this book to protect the privacy of individuals.

ACKNOWLEDGMENTS

First, I give honor to God who is truly the head and love of my life. Without Him, this book would not have been completed.

I also thank God for my wonderful parents, Benjamin and Hoseanna Diggs. I'm grateful that God allowed me to be produced through you. You guys are amazing!

To my sisters and brother, Rodney, Keisha, and Kia, I love you all dearly. We may not see eye-to-eye on some things, and we may get on each other's last nerve, but I'm grateful to have siblings like you. I couldn't have asked for anyone better.

To my nieces and nephews, Dacia, Daron, Darius, Peyton, Darrien, Emmai, Elyssa, Xavier, and Elaina – Auntie Kendra loves you. You are so special; you were placed on this earth for such a time and a season.

To my godfamily, Sis Jeanne, KC, Kris, Shanell, Kaleb, Madisyn, and my godsons CJ and Clark Kent. To my aunts, uncles, and cousins, I am blessed to have you all in my life. Love you.

To one of my best friends, Charisse Beverly, thank you for your sincere sisterhood and support on this long journey I have had with this book and along the way. Thank you for your efforts and your hard work formatting and editing the first draft of my book. You are awesome.

To my other friends, Jewel, Ivory, Keinisha, and Christian, I love you guys dearly; you are the best gal friends anyone could have

To my church family, Evangel and Zion Place, my leaders, mentors, the late Bishop Otis Lockett Sr., Pastor O, and First Lady Lockett, thank you for your heart for the people of God and having a desire to see us grow to our maximum potential. Love you dearly.

To my drill sergeant, friend, and coach, Robert, thank you for seeing the warrior in me and still bringing her out. Thank you for not giving up on me.

To my PUSH/ AWOL Fitness family, I thank God every day for such a place that has truly helped groom me to grow. You guys rock!!

To my MAC family, I love you guys! I truly do. Thank you for helping me to perfect my artistry and grow into the leader I am.

My clients, especially Antonina Griffin, thank you for supporting me over and over again. You saw greatness at the beginning and for that I'm grateful.

Sis Sharon Johnson and Olivia, thank you for opening your heart to me. Thank you for being rainbows in my cloud. Thank you for being a listening ear, supportive of where I am going, and seeing greatness in me.

And to every person who will support and read this book, I truly appreciate and thank you for taking the time to read it. I hope it blesses and encourages you.

I dedicate this book to all the women and men trying to find themselves and their purpose in the world. Be who God created you to be. Walk in His power.

"For we are God's masterpiece. He has created us anew in Christ Jesus, so we can do the good things he planned for us long ago" (Ephesians 2:10 - NLT).

HIS MASTERPIECE

FOREWORD

Kendra is a woman that God has given beauty for ashes. She has overcome great trials and has exemplified what it means to be more than a conqueror. God is shaping and molding her into something special! After reading "His Masterpiece: A Royal Journey of Self Discovery in God", every reader is sure to gain strength and encouragement. It's a must read for everyone going through metamorphosis.

Supt. Otis Lockett, Jr.
Evangel Fellowship COGIC, Greensboro, NC

TABLE OF CONTENTS

Introduction 1
Chapter 1: I Am Special 9
Chapter 2: I Am Gorgeous 17
Chapter 3: I Am Gifted 23
Chapter 4: I Am Important 31
Chapter 5: I Am One in a Million 37
Chapter 6: I Am a Star 43
Chapter 7: I Am Loved 47
Chapter 8: I Am Happy 55
Chapter 9: I Am Sacred 61
Chapter 10: I Am Protected 65
Chapter 11: I Am Fearless 71
Chapter 12: I am Capable 77
Chapter 13: I am Resilient 81
Chapter 14: I Am Determined 89
Chapter 15: I Am Well 95
Chapter 16: I Am Strong 101
Chapter 17: I Am Enough 107
Chapter 18: I Am Unshakable 115
Conclusion: I Am Royalty 123

His Masterpiece

INTRODUCTION

Diggs Household
Sunday Morning, October 1989
Kendra's Christening

"Hoseanna! Have you seen my belt?" my husband yelled across the hallway. It was a typical Sunday morning, and we were getting ready for church.

"It should be in the closet, Tony," I said hurriedly as I applied my chocolate raspberry lipstick and finished my hair. As I grabbed my spritz bottle, Tony came into the bathroom pulling his belt through the holes to secure it.

I looked at my husband with admiration. I couldn't believe we had produced three beautiful girls. We had faced a lot and come a long way from when we lived in Virginia. But no matter what, we were determined to be together. Tony looked at me, kissed me gently on the cheek, and exited the bathroom.

"Mommy!" a small voice whined. "Keisha ate my breakfast!" Kia said with her eyes full of tears.

Keisha ran in right behind her. "I did not!" she protested in direct conflict with the evidence around her mouth and on the top of her dress.

I sighed. "Keisha and Kia stop fussing and get ready for church."

"But Mommy! Keisha ate my food!" Kia kept whining.

I shook my head. *My girls*. They were a handful. "Go and get dressed."

Both of them walked away still fussing.

I went into my room to grab a pair of earrings and heard a soft cooing. It was my baby girl Kendra. I walked over to the crib and glanced at her. She looked just like her father — eyes, lips, and all. I had already dressed her in an adorable white outfit for her very special day; she was getting christened. I wasn't able to do that for my other girls, but I made sure I did it for her.

"Are you almost ready, Hoseanna? Melvin and Toni will be meeting us here any minute now," said my husband as he grabbed the baby bag and car keys.

"Yes, I am. Please, make sure Keisha and Kia are ready."

I paused, smiled, and said to him, "You are looking mighty sexy in that suit." Then I chuckled and winked. My husband just smiled back and shook his head.

The doorbell rang. "Uncle Melvin and Aunt Toni are here!" Keisha screamed as she opened the door.

A slightly older version of my husband walked in. *Geez, those Diggs genes are strong.*

"Uncle Melvin!" Keisha and Kia shouted in unison as they ran to the door.

"Y'all almost knocked me down! Wow, you girls are growing up!" Melvin exclaimed.

I came downstairs with Kendra, and we all made small talk as we headed outside.

"Oh, Hosie, your girls are growing up. They are just blossoming!" my sister-in-law shrieked with excitement.

"Yes, I love my girls," I said proudly.

My sis-in-law looked at me with admiration. "Hosie, girl, where did you get that dress from? That's a bad dress!"

I blushed. "Well, thank you, sis. Just a little something I picked up at the Carolina Circle Mall," I said as I twirled and winked.

We giggled as we got into our separate cars. I made sure Kendra was secure in the backseat with Keisha and Kia. Then I hopped in the front seat of our red Nissan and sped out of the driveway with Melvin and Toni following. We turned onto Balboa Street, the home of Evangel Fellowship Church of God in Christ. Joyous music of praise and worship could be heard coming from the inside of the building.

Our church was beautiful with purple pews and floral carpeting. We loved our leaders, Pastor Otis and Barbara Lockett; we were blessed to have them. They truly wanted God's best for our lives.

We all walked in and the ushers directed us to our seats. I saw my best friend Jeanne and her husband Cornell waiting for us. They are Kendra's godparents. Jeanne grabbed me and gave me a hug. "Why, don't you look fancy today. Who's getting christened, you or Kendra?" she said with a chuckle.

"Oh, hush girl," I laughed as I popped her hand. I gave Kendra to her and looked around to see if my other family members had shown up yet. Just as I was beginning to lose hope, I saw my niece, Esther and felt immediate relief. I wondered why I was so nervous.

The mass choir got up and sang a beautiful selection called "Perfect Peace." That song moved my spirit to tears as Brother Terry Staton sang the lead perfectly. He could sing his behind off.

My heart started to race. It was time.

A man with smooth, dark skin, a mustache, a bald head with some hair on the sides, and a million-dollar smile approached the podium. It was Pastor Lockett. He called forth both sides of the families present for the christening: mine and Tony's. As Pastor Lockett prayed over us, I held my baby girl close, but my mind couldn't stop racing with questions. I couldn't help but wonder what she would grow up to be. I wondered what type of impact she would make on this world.

"Honey, you have to hand Kendra to me now," Tony whispered interrupting my thoughts.

"Oh, I'm sorry," I said, startled. I handed her over to him. Kendra was fast asleep in his arms, oblivious of all that was happening around her. A little snore even came from her nose.

Pastor Lockett approached us and smiled. "Come on, Kendra," he said as he grabbed her. "She looks just like Keisha," he chuckled. He walked to the pulpit, held her up, and started to pray. "Even though I'm asleep, my heart waketh.

And even now, Lord, as I hold Kendra up to You, You said if we believe in our hearts and confess with our mouths, we shall be saved. Kendra will believe unto righteousness with her heart and with her mouth confessions will be made unto salvation.

And, if we call on Your name, we shall be saved. Thank You for her godly parents, Father, let her see the glory of Jesus. When she reaches the age of accountability let there will be no difficulty in giving her life unto You. Let these instructions be sealed in her spirit and her mind.

Let the Spirit of God bring them back to her remembrance. May Your anointing rest on her. And, from this day, may You endow her with Your Spirit and blessings. The Lord says, 'She shall grow up and, yea, she shall be somewhat strange in thine sight, but it is only because of me, for I have put My seal upon her. And, yea, I have already put My instructions in her. But I say to you, parents, do not make her go in the way that you would have her to go.

Ask for My discernment, and I will show you what I will make of her. Then I will give you wisdom on the way she should go, and she will not depart from it. I will bless this child and through her many shall be blessed.' Now, Lord, we dedicate her to You for Your glory."

As he walked down the steps, the pastor gave Kendra back to my husband. I treasured everything he said in my heart. What would she have to face in life? What adversities would she have to overcome? Would she have to be broken to see her greatness? Who knows if she was born for such a time as this?

His Masterpiece

Chapter 1

I AM SPECIAL

On June 27, 1989, at 9:13 p.m., I entered the world. My mother told me I came out of the womb whining and looking around. I suppose I was curious, even as a newborn. My mother worked in retail and cosmetics for years, and my father has worked for the United States Postal Service for as long as I can remember. I'm the youngest of four children; my siblings are my brother Rodney and my sisters, Keisha and Kia, I am the baby girl or "the spoiled brat" as Kia would say jokingly.

My mother and father are the best parents a daughter could have. Their marriage isn't perfect, but they love each other. My dad spoiled my mum and still does to this very day. I wanted my future husband to be just like my father.

My parents have always been very involved in ministry at Evangel. My father is a deacon, and my mother was on the praise team and a part of the prayer team. They also both sang in the mass choir. Needless to say, I was definitely a church baby; all I knew was the church. We lived at 2916 Dove Street in a two-story sky-blue house with three bedrooms, one bathroom, a basement, and a laundry room. You can imagine the chaos in the morning with four females trying to get ready in that house. Our neighborhood was quiet, and we had great neighbors. We didn't live that far from Claremont Homes, which was considered "the hood," so my mother would caution us to never go down there. However, despite my mother's warnings, my sisters would disobey and go there to hang with their friends. They were a bit more adventurous than I was.

I genuinely believe that Jesus and my mom are best friends because He would reveal everything to her that we were trying to do in secret. Her spirit of discernment is very strong. Even now as a grown woman, I'm scared to lie to her because I know she can see right through me. There were certain rules we had in the house, but one *certain* rule was not to listen to secular music or, in my mother's words, "put demonic people on our walls" (posters of rappers or singers). But thanks to my sisters, we would sneak and listen to 102 JAMZ. I learned a few songs. To cover our tracks, we always changed the station on the radio back to gospel Music.

As a young girl, I was obsessed with Barbie dolls, books, Barney, tutus, and playing in makeup. I was quite prissy. One time, I got in trouble for doing my face with my mom's makeup. Lipstick, false lashes, and eyeliner were everywhere. Thank God, we didn't have social media back then!

At Evangel Daycare, my preschool teacher, Sister Valerie was my favorite. I was always with her. I was a bit of a loner, so she would try to get me involved in activities with other children. I really didn't want to, but I did it to make her happy. One day, a group of girls and I went to play on the slide. I was terrified and hesitant, so I cried.

I ran to Sis. Valerie and grabbed her leg. The group of girls laughed and teased me. "Scaredy cat, scaredy cat," they sang. I cried and ran away. The girls were eventually put in time out. *Why don't they like me?* I asked myself. *I just want us to be friends, but they pick on me.* I don't think I ever understood why children could be so cruel, but as I got older, the teasing got worse.

By the age of 7, I was a hefty girl. I was beginning to hit puberty at a very early age; I couldn't run away from it. My mother and sisters matured early, too. As a matter of fact, all of the women on both sides of my family hit puberty at a young age.

The first time I went shopping for a training bra with my mother, I was very embarrassed. With tears in my eyes, I whined to my mother, "I don't want to do this, mommy; I don't want to grow up. Why do I need a bra now?"

My mother turned to me, "Kendra, it's going to be alright. You are growing into a young lady. Don't be afraid," she said as she kissed me on the cheek. I still hated it. My body was changing, and I had to get used to being different from the other girls in my class.

By the age of 8, my body was truly that of a woman, but then, much to my dismay, it got worse. One night, I woke up feeling heavy. I got up and went to the bathroom, flicked on the light, and sat down, but all I saw was blood. "Mommy!" I screamed hysterically.

My parents jumped from their bed and ran to the bathroom. My dad came in and his eyes got huge. "Hoseanna, you need to come quickly."

My mother rushed into the bathroom and looked at me with her eyes full of tears. "My baby, my baby!" she cried as she embraced me. She helped me clean up and washed my sheets.

I stayed home from school that day. My godmother, Sis Jeanne, my godsisters KC and Kris, my aunt Kay, my cousin Esther, and my grandmother all came to the house. It was weird being the center of attention. My grandmother grabbed a tissue for my mother, rubbed her back, and said, "Hosie, stop all that crying. You are acting the same way you did when Keisha and Kia got their cycles."

My mother let out a deep breath. "I know, Momma. I'm just not ready for her to grow up."

I stayed in bed all day, but everyone kept looking at me to see if I was okay. It was very awkward.

The next day at school, my mother gave a note to my teacher, Mrs. Moore. She kept looking at me throughout the day and asking me if I had to go to the bathroom. I told her no every time. However, during lunch, I finally had to go.

"Are you okay?" one of my classmates asked me as she analyzed my body. "You're not sick, are you?" she said as her face scrunched up.

"I'm fine," I said hurriedly. I put my lunch tray down, and I ran to the bathroom. As I was running, I tripped and the sanitary napkins fell out my bag and sprawled across the hallway — in front of the fifth graders. I gasped and ran over to grab them.

One girl screamed, "EWWWW! Whose are these?" Then she and all of the other fifth graders started laughing.

I was devastated. Mortified, I ran into the bathroom and cried.

I was an easy target to pick on. I was a hefty girl with the fully developed body of a woman. "Miss

Piggy" was one of the cruel nicknames other students ascribed to me. Once, in art class, our teacher gave us free time and one of my classmates drew me with large circles on the chest and a big circle for the stomach. Everyone in my class laughed at me. I didn't say much after that; I stayed to myself. *Don't they realize I just want to be friends?*

I went home and cried to my mother. She comforted me, but she was angry. "I'm tired of these girls messing with my baby," my mother exclaimed. "I'm going to that school tomorrow!"

My sister, Kia, interjected, "Do you need me to handle these nappy-headed girls?" she roared. "I'm not afraid to handle anybody who messes with my sister." She started punching her hand.

My mother gave her the evil eye. "Kia, sit down! I'll handle this."

Kia and I were like oil and water, just like all siblings can be. We fought over everything, but if anyone messed with me, she was always ready to beat someone up.

The next morning, my mother followed through on her promise and came with me to school. She and the principal exchanged words.

After a 30-minute talk, she walked out of the principal's office. She looked at me with sincerity in her eyes and said, "Don't you let these girls get to you. You are beautiful and special. Don't you ever forget that."

HIS MASTERPIECE

Chapter 2

I AM GORGEOUS

I always walked around with my head down. I would close my eyes and look away during conversations. Naturally, I was shy but bubbly at the same time.

However, I had an especially difficult time in the third grade. I already felt like an outcast because I was so different physically. Not only did I struggle socially but academically as well.

One day, as I was walking down the hallway, a woman with a short, black, pixie haircut, Bohemian clothes, charm bracelets, and pointed, sharp nails, walked right in front of me. With her rich foreign accent, she smiled and said, "Why are you walking with your head down?" Her sharp, hazel eyes glared into my soul.

I looked up and replied, "I don't know. I just don't feel like looking up."

She cocked her head to the side. "Don't you know that you are a queen? Queens never hold their heads down," she said as she lifted my chin higher. "I'm your Guidance Counselor's aid, and I think I would like to see you more often."

She observed me some more and smiled again. "Remember who you are, beautiful. I'll be seeing you soon," she said with a wink and walked away.

I reflected on what she said. *A queen? Me? She can't be serious!* I sighed and walked back to class.

A few days later, she kept her word. I was in her office with several girls from my class. I was more at peace there with her than in my class; it was my escape. I loved going to her office.

She even taught us how to walk. "Heads up and chest out. Walk like the queens you are," she stated as she walked toward me and lifted my chin higher. She smiled, and I smiled back at her. I couldn't believe she saw any type of royalty in me.

As the school years progressed, I noticed that I kept getting attention from little boys in my class. Especially this one boy. His name was Jake, and he was *bad;* he always had a devilish grin on his face. One day, my class went outside to play. Jake and his homies were scheming. That day, we were running track. The next thing I knew, I was on the ground; he tripped me. All of his friends chuckled.

"Jake! I'm telling on you!" I screamed.

He turned and with a sinister look, he said, "I don't care. Tell, but I hope you don't run out of breath with those big jugs you have."

I paused and turned around. They were all still laughing.

I was getting tired of him. I had to figure out a way to get him back ASAP. The following week, we were outside again. I saw Jake out of the corner of my eye. *He's up to something.* My mind ran as I was turning the jump rope.

"Kendra! You almost made me fall!" my classmate sneered.

"Oh, I'm sorry. I think Jake is plotting something," I replied.

With her hand on her hip, she confidently stated, "Jake likes you. My mommy said boys do crazy things when they like you."

My eyebrows frowned up. "I don't believe that," I retorted. "If you like someone, why hurt them?"

Suddenly, I felt a hand grab one of my breasts tightly and a slap on my behind. It was Jake! In an uncharacteristic rage, I dropped the jump rope and ran after him. As I chased him, he was laughing hysterically. When I finally caught up to him, I jumped on him and shouted, "Don't you ever touch me again!" His eyes were huge, and he still had his signature evil sneer.

"Okay. I won't do it again."

A loud whistle blew. It was our teacher, Ms. Peak. "What's going here?" she asked. "Mrs. Peak...he —" I stammered.

Before I got a word out, she yelled, "Kendra! Jake! Classroom now!"

I was very upset and hoped I wasn't going to get into trouble. We had to sit in the classroom for the remainder of the recess. I opened my book and tried to read, while he banged on his desk with pencils. *Gosh, was he annoying.*

Later on, that day, my father picked me up. "How was school?" he asked.

"It was okay. I'm just ready to go home," I replied. I never mentioned what happened to me to anyone; not even my mom. I didn't want to make them upset.

I have always cherished having peace around; I liked being the peacemaker. But I knew I was going to have to deal with life, whether I liked it or not.

HIS MASTERPIECE

Chapter 3

I AM GIFTED

As I got older, I felt less isolated and left out. Many of my female classmates were beginning to look like me. My grades had improved and, overall, I was happy. My fifth-grade teacher Mrs. Cobbs was my favorite. She had a beautiful, brown complexion, a sassy haircut, and always wore the cutest outfits. Mrs. Cobbs was a ball of energy who, coincidentally, also taught my older sisters and matriculated in high school with my mother. She taught us to believe in and love ourselves no matter what.

Back then, I had a close-knit group of girlfriends. Within the group of five, I was definitely a follower; I hated to be in the spotlight. Close to the end of the school year, Mrs. Cobbs decided that we should put on a talent show as there were several skilled students in our class. My friends and I decided to do something together for the show. While planning the performance on the phone, I chimed in, "Maybe we should sing or dance."

"Who asked you?" one girl hissed back at me. "No one asked for your input, Kendra. I make the decisions."

I quietly replied, "Geez, okay. I just thought we could sing or —"

She interrupted me again. "Like I said, Kendra, shut up!"

Suddenly, I heard another voice on the phone. It was my older sister Kia. "Who do you think you are talking to my sister like this? I'm tired of you fake, nappy-headed girls talking to my sister any kind of way!" she screamed into the phone. "Either you are going to respect my baby sister or I'm coming to Bessemer Elementary myself, and you don't want that!"

The phone was silent. After several moments, they replied, "No ma'am," in unison.

Shocked, I hung up the phone. My sister came into my room and shouted, "You don't need friends like that. You are better off alone."

The next day, the girls didn't even look my way. It was hurtful, but there was nothing I could really do. I stayed to myself.

Towards the end of the school year, Mrs. Cobbs asked me to sing in front of the class. Terrified, I stated, "Mrs. Cobbs, I can't do this."

She looked at me and smiled. "Get 'can't' out of your vocabulary. I know you can. Plus, you're a Diggs. Everyone in your family sings," she laughed.

Back then my favorite movie was "Our Friend Martin." I was obsessed with it and watched it almost every day. I knew the dialogue, songs, and everything else by rote. It is an animated film about a young, black boy and his friends traveling back in time to the Civil Rights Era and meeting Martin Luther King Jr. They had a lot of adventures. That movie actually inspired my love of Black History; I even wanted to become a Black History teacher. In addition to watching the movie incessantly, I also listened to the soundtrack and, in particular, the song "Peace in the World" by Shanice Williams. Despite it being a difficult song, I endeavored to perform it for the class.

Finally, the day for the talent show was here. Mrs. Cobbs decided to put both fifth-grade classes together, which made me even more nervous. I opted to wear a black faux leather suit with studs on the collar and pant legs. Even though I routinely sang at church, I had never performed in front of my classmates. I belted out the song with my eyes clenched closed. At the end of the song, I apprehensively opened my eyes. Much to my surprise, other students and teachers from different grades had crowded the doorway. A thunderous applause shook the classroom. My teacher hugged me; I felt so loved.

After my performance, I locked eyes with a boy named Deitrick. He was in the other fifth-grade class. He had cinnamon brown skin, dark almond-shaped eyes with long eyelashes, and thick, wavy hair. He looked like a dark-skinned Bruno Mars. If you don't think Bruno is cute, something is truly wrong with you. Just kidding! *Is this what it feels like to have a crush*? I wondered. I blushed as he smiled at me.

After class, he came up to me and said, "I loved your song. It was nice." He smiled again, and I smiled back.

"Thank you." I giggled.

"I'll see you tomorrow," he said to me.

My face was flushed. I just didn't know what to do with myself.

The next day at recess, Deitrick approached me on the playground. He took me by the hand and led me to the swings where he pushed me back and forth. I giggled hysterically. Next, we played on the monkey bars and then we got on the slide. We both slid down and ran under the slide.

He peered at me with his beautiful eyes, and my heart started to beat out of my chest. He moved in close to my face and gently placed his soft lips onto mine. It was my first kiss.

I was completely lost in the moment. He then kissed me on the cheek and whispered gently in my ear, "You're very pretty."

I had never received a compliment from a boy before. As I leaned in to give him another a kiss, I heard a voice squeal, "Oooooooooooohhhhhhhh, I'm telling Mrs. Cobbs!" Then the girl ran off.

"Wait!" I gulped. "Please, don't tell!" The girl was already gone. *Man, am I in trouble.* Number one, I wasn't supposed to have a boyfriend, let alone let him kiss me. Mrs. Cobbs told me to come to the class, and I told her what happened. Thank God, she let it slide.

My mother, on the other hand, was another story. Jesus and my mom must've had a conversation because, by the time I got home, she was asking a lot of unusual questions. It should be noted that I'm not a good liar. "Why are you so chippy today?" my mom inquired as she sat down at the table.

"Nothing, Mom. Can't I just be happy?" I stammered.

She looked at me intensely. "Is it a boy?" she inquired as she got closer and closer to me.

"No...mom...well...yeah," I stuttered with my head down.

"Did he kiss you?"

By this point, she was leering at me. "Yes," I whispered.

"What? I can't hear you!" she replied.

I sighed. "Yes, Mom. He did kiss me on the lips and the cheek, and he said I was pretty," I said with a massive exhale.

"Did he touch you?" my mother asked with seriousness in her voice.

"No!" I screamed. "He just kissed me."

My mother sat in the chair and looked at me. "You know our rules about boys/boyfriends. No boys until we think you are ready."

Tears filled my eyes, "I know, Mommy," I whimpered. Dejected, I retreated upstairs to my room and wept.

On the last day of school, the fifth-grade classes were combined again. Deitrick sat beside me. I had a sad look on my face. "Everything okay?" he questioned.

I turned to him and said, "I can't talk to you anymore. My mom said I'm not ready for friends that are boys or boyfriends. I'm sorry."

He looked at me, nodded his head and gave me a hug. Then, he got up and walked away. It was like a part of my heart left with him, but I guess Moms know best.

Later that summer, my big sisters and I walked to the library up the street. At that time, it was my favorite place to hang out, so I was trying to get there as quickly as possible. On the way, I saw a friend of mine with Deitrick. They were hugging and kissing each other. Something broke in me. My heart shattered. *Why do the worst things happen to me?*

HIS MASTERPIECE

Chapter 4

I AM IMPORTANT

I was a little older, a little wiser, and considered the "old soul" in my group of friends. Even back then, I didn't look my age as I've always looked a little older than what I was. My interest was in doing makeup. I watched my mother do hers all the time.

"When can I start wearing makeup? I wanna learn," I insisted. "Not yet," my mom said. "Clear lip gloss is all you're getting."

I turned away sorrowfully. Eventually, she started letting me wear mascara and colored lip glosses from CoverGirl.

I wanted to participate in the youth service at my church. All the other kids my age was involved, so I wanted to be a part of it too. Initially, my mother didn't want me to be in the youth group because, sad to say, the Devil can be right in the church as well. However, the youth pastors, John and Tasha Hill, reassured my mother I would be okay under their care. Once I joined,

I was actually happy. I felt protected under them. I got involved in the praise team, youth choir, and even started attending some of the youth services. One night, after my youth pastor preached his heart-wrenching sermon, I decided in my heart to get saved and give my life to God. I knew that being saved was important. I couldn't play religion anymore; I had to get serious about developing that relationship.

By this time, I was a bit smaller, and I was growing into a young woman. I didn't eat as much. I was getting thinner, and I liked the way I looked. However, I wanted to slim down faster, so I would intentionally starve myself. I wouldn't eat, and if I did, it would be a very small meal immediately followed by laxatives. I had very poor self-esteem; I didn't see myself as anything. When my mother found out what I was doing, she was shocked.

"What is wrong with you?" she fretted. "Don't you know this could've done more harm than good? Kendra, you have to stop this! Enough is enough!" Then she faced me toward the mirror. "Don't you realize how beautiful you are?" she stated as she held my face.

I bowed my head. I read the Bible and knew we were created in God's image, but why didn't I believe that?

One Sunday night after evening service, I was walking towards the door when Sister Theresa motioned for me to come to her. I gave her the biggest hug and she held me by the hand. She looked at me intently. "Remember, Kendra, you are beautiful, not only on the outside but the inside too. You are a gorgeous girl, and that's why there are a lot of girls jealous of you. Be careful who you call your friends," she advised me.

Jealous of me? Who? Am I really that threatening? I'm just Kendra. I thought to myself. It's crazy how people can have a view of you or be jealous of you for no reason.

My high school days were definitely an adventure. I went to Page High School. I met my best friend, in the tenth and eleventh grades, respectively. I was in a drama team called the Page Playmakers. I was also in chorus. Theatre and music were my passions. Even so, there was still a part of me that didn't feel accepted. I always felt like the oddball out. A particular group of girls in my youth group were very popular, and I just wanted to be accepted and win their approval.

One summer, my youth group went to "Six Flags Over Georgia" in Atlanta. It was lots of fun. However, an upsetting incident occurred while we were there. This group of girls decided to confront me and tell me about myself. I never really spent time with them as we were not friends. I knew that I was highly sensitive and because I had been sheltered for half of my life there were certain things that I was not accustomed to. Admittedly, I whined and complained about things that I found to be irritating. After I returned from the restroom, I saw them sitting down at the table facing me. I went over and asked, "Is everything okay?"

The leader of the girls said to me, "We are just tired of you, Kendra. You have been complaining about so many unnecessary things." All of the girls nodded in agreement.

My eyes burned with tears. "Well, why do you guys have to come to me in the group, not individually? Plus, you were all complaining about stuff, too."

Another girl raised her voice up a decibel. "We felt like you wouldn't have taken us as seriously. Plus, this is not about us; it's about you."

I shook my head. Tears rolled down my face. "This is an attack on me. I feel like you could've approached me individually. I don't appreciate this whatsoever." I cried and ran away. As I was fleeing, I bumped into my youth pastor.

"Is everything okay?" he inquired with a look of concern on his face.

"Yes, sir. I'm fine," I replied as I wiped the tears from my face.

On our way back to Greensboro, I was quiet. Thoughts kept running through my mind. *Why don't they like me? Am I that annoying? Am I that sensitive? Just forget it! I'm going to be by myself.* I could've tried to apologize for my actions and tried to be friends with them, but in my mind, I didn't see any amends.

A few Sundays later, we had evening service. My mother forced me to sit with her. Even though they didn't care for me, I still wanted to be with them. I felt so alone. A guest speaker ministered that night. I wasn't paying much attention, and I played it off well by scanning through my Bible. When it was time to give an offering, I walked with my mother and father. Then I heard the guest speaker say, "Stop! You, right there! Lift your hands!" I looked around, and he was staring at me. "You walk like a queen and that's exactly who you are. God calls you a queen."

Tears started to roll down my face. The saints were applauding. My dad had to grab my mom because she was about to take off running in the church. I forgot what else was said, but he laid his hands on me, and I fell to the floor. After I came to, I returned to my seat. I noticed that the girls were all staring at me, which made me quite uncomfortable. Nevertheless, I didn't show it. I sat there with a smile on my face. I guess Psalm 23 was right in saying, "He will prepare a table in the presence of my enemies."

HIS MASTERPIECE

Chapter 5

I AM ONE IN A MILLION

I loved the Lord, and I proclaimed to be a Christian but I still wanted to have fun. Everyone knew that I was a Christian. As a matter of fact, one of my nicknames was Ms. Holy Ghost. I had never been in a successful relationship. I would try to sneak and date, but it never worked out in my favor. I was dumped, cheated on or my mother and father would find out and cut off the relationship.

I was quite fond of one of the drummers at my church. Paul was his name. Actually, I was crazy about him, but that didn't turn out the way I wanted. As a matter of fact, there were a lot of incidents with guys that never turned out favorably. Once, I was at the library up the street from my house with Mark. He was holding me from behind. My sister caught us and yelled at me in front of everyone in the library. Not only was I mortified, but I got in huge trouble when I got home. It sucked. Eventually, around my junior and senior year, my mother and father were less strict with me.

My twelfth grade English teacher, Mr. Brown, was an older, black gentleman with a bald head and big eyes; he wore glasses. He was another favorite teacher of mine. To pass his class, you had to follow two simple rules: be quiet and do your work. I was his aid in class. I would check everyone into class and return to my assigned seat. There was a guy who sat across from me. He had chocolate skin and a bright, white smile. His name was Taj. He was from Africa, Eventually, we started talking, and he invited me to be his date for prom.

When the big night arrived, I was elated. I wore a candy apple red dress that my mother bought me from Fashion Town. Keisha styled my hair, and I did my own makeup. After years of begging my mother to teach me makeup, she finally relented. "Okay, I'm going to teach you *one* time," she emphasized. I gleaned as much as I could from that tutorial, and I ran with it!

"Are you excited?" Keisha asked as she was putting the finishing touches on my hair. I smiled and replied, "Yes, I am," butI was worried. I know traditionally on prom night; a lot of girls give up their goodies. I had discussed with him that we were not doing anything. "I'm a virgin, and I want to wait until marriage," I said to him with seriousness in my eyes.

He threw his head back. "A man has needs," he joked, but he knew I was serious. He arrived quite late to pick me up and offered no explanation as to why.

My mom was snapping pictures of me as I walked down the stairs dressed to the nines. He and I took a quick picture together, and we were on our way. "Don't try anything stupid!" my sisters yelled in unison as we walked to the car. He shook his head in agreement with them and closed my door. Then we sped out the driveway.

When we arrived, I saw a lot of my friends and classmates. While I was taking pictures with them, he was eerily quiet. I whispered and asked if he was okay. He nodded his head. We took our picture and danced. At the end of the night, I thought that we would go out to eat or hang out. Apparently, he had other plans; he took me home and sped off. I later found out that he went to an after party with two other girls who were known for giving it up easily. I was hurt, but I kept my standard.

Graduation was upon me. I was so excited. Keisha gave me a full sew in with two packs of 14-inch hair in my head. You couldn't tell me "nothing" with my full Chinese bang; I *knew* I was fly! My best friend Khadijah came to the house. "Congratulations, best friend!" she said cheerfully.

"Thank you, best friend," I giggled. She had graduated a year before me and was at A&T getting her degree in teaching.

Graduation was a blast. Seeing my family, friends, and classmates was amazing. I felt as if it were a dream. High school was finally over. We had Senior Night after graduation. I won a TV, $200, and I got my picture drawn. One of my classmates jeered me saying, "You don't need that TV. Aren't Christians not supposed to watch ungodly things?" He snickered.

I rolled my eyes. "Shut up!" I said jokingly as I grabbed my TV. It was great spending time with my classmates one final time before we went our separate ways.

That summer, I got a job at Ross. Although I didn't have much experience, they gave me a chance. My dream job was to become a MAC Girl. I knew I was inexperienced, but I kept trying. I was impressed with how unique and cool they were. I loved to observe them. They were so fierce; I wanted to be like them. I wound up having a lot of consecutive, short-term jobs. I went from Ross to Dillard's to being a nanny for my aunt.

While I was working at Dillard's, I had a boyfriend. He was much older than me. I was 18, and he was 26. I knew the relationship wouldn't last long, and he eventually dumped me. We were just too different. I was young and naive.

My heart was really in makeup. I wanted to have the title of Professional Makeup Artist under my belt. I knew I ultimately wanted to be a MAC Girl, so I did what I had to do. I became a fragrance model/rep for Parlux Fragrances. My friend Tika and I rocked it out in Belk. A lot of people liked us and our attention-getting techniques. We were a pretty good team. I made good money with Parlux, but my heart still craved to be a makeup artist.

One day, I was walking through the mall, and I saw a sign saying, "Now Hiring Makeup Artists, Licensed Estheticians, Cosmetologists, and Salespeople." The company was called Bovanti Cosmetics. I immediately wrote the email down and told Tika about it. "What's the worst that can happen? Girl, you got this! You never know; they may email you back tonight!" Tika declared. She boosted my confidence.

That evening when I got home, I emailed my resume to them. Apparently, she was right because the next morning, I got a response. It was from Malika Bouvet one of the owners of the makeup boutique in Greensboro. My dreams were coming true; I was going to be a makeup artist.

HIS MASTERPIECE

Chapter 6

I AM A STAR

Bovanti Cosmetics was a huge stepping stone into the makeup world. If anyone asks me how I got started, I always give credit to them and to my mother. They really helped me to perfect my blending techniques. If something was not blended correctly, they would tell us to do it again. "We are about excellence. Perfected practice makes perfect," Mrs. Bouvet would say.

Malika and Mandisa were the owners of the boutique in Greensboro and also the daughters of the presidents. Malika focused on the business aspects of the company, while Mandisa dealt with the artistic side. They made a great team.

My job was challenging, but I learned a lot about myself and my skills as an artist. Despite those positive strides, I still struggled with my confidence. They saw more potential in me than I saw in myself. The biggest honor was working with them at the Bronner Bros Show in Atlanta. It was so exciting. Seeing the myriads of hairstyles and makeup was amazing; it was a beauty fantasyland.

While working for Bovanti, I met someone at the mall. His name was Craig. He was a chocolate brother. As you can see, I have a thing for chocolate guys. He was a Christian, and he attended a church I was familiar with. My parents knew his pastor and first lady very well. I knew deep down in my heart that he was going to be my husband. I frequently went to his church and even developed great relationships with his friends and family. We spent time together, took pictures, and overall, he was a great guy to be around. Unexpectedly, however, things started to slow down. He sat me down to talk. It felt surreal when I heard the words come out of his mouth. "Kendra, this is just not working. We need to break up."

Those words burned my soul. I went home and stared at the mirror. "What is wrong with me? Why do I always get dumped? Am I ugly? Am I undesirable?" I shuddered at the sight of myself, and I wailed. That situation triggered my emotional eating, and I fell into a depression. I shaved off my eyebrows and cried myself to sleep. I desperately wanted the same type of love my parents had for each other, but it constantly evaded me.

My mother was quite upset about the breakup and, as usual, tried to come to the rescue. "Mom, please," I cried. "I already feel bad enough; don't make it worse." My mom didn't listen to anything I said. She called the first lady of his church, and they had a long talk. A few days later, I saw Craig glaring at me at the mall. I was still hurt, but I had to move on.

A couple of months passed, and I was back in a better place emotionally. I was content. I felt the happiest when I was doing makeup or when I was in ministry. By this time, I was a worship leader at Zion Place Ministries. Bishop Lockett was the type of man who would send you to another ministry if he felt it was time for you to go and grow somewhere else. That's precisely what happened to me.

We were a great praise team. We traveled to several places together and ministered. They would always push me out of my comfort zone. As Zion Place Ministries progressed, a lot of new members started to come, but one particular member caught my eye. He looked really good with smooth, brown skin, thick eyebrows, smooth mustache, earrings in his ears, and his Express button-up shirt. He would watch me every time I sang or led a song. He would even watch me when I went to the front for the offering. One Sunday, we bumped into each other. A smile parted his lips. "Hey, my name is Javad."

HIS MASTERPIECE

Chapter 7

I AM LOVED

"Well, it's nice to meet you," I said as I noticed the little gap in his teeth. "Javad, that's pretty unique," I said.

"My mother named me," he remarked with a flirtatious smile. I looked down and said, "Oh, my bad. I wasn't trying to insult your name. Speaking of which, my name is Kendra."

"Nice to meet you officially. Well, I have to go now. I'll see you at Bible study." Then he walked away. There was just something about him that piqued my interest and intrigued me.

A few days later, I saw him at the mall and waved him over. He smiled and walked over to where I was standing outside the door at work. "Is this where you work?" he asked as he admired the store.

"Yep, sure is," I replied. He cocked his head to the side and said, "Hmmm, no wonder your makeup is always nice."

I started to blush. I had never received a compliment from a man about my makeup before. It gave me butterflies. "Thank you," I beamed. I noticed a bag of women's shoes in his hand.

"Oh, this is for my mom. I'm headed out of town for the holidays," he replied. "Oh okay," I said. "So that means you're not coming to the end of the year banquet for ZP?" I questioned. I really wanted him to be there.

He nodded his head. "Yes, I'll be there," he replied. "Awesome," I said with a smile. We waved goodbye.

As soon as I got off from work, I jumped on my computer and logged into Facebook. I could've been a private investigator because I did a thorough search for his name. After a few minutes, I finally found him. I looked at his picture and bio. I saw he went to an engineering school. *Fine and smart.* I sent him a friend request, and a few hours later, he approved me. We exchanged numbers. He texted me and called me more than I called him. I never had a guy chase me before, and it felt good to be pursued. I was happy to be on someone's mind.

Zion Place's End of the Year Banquet was later that weekend. I felt beautiful that night with my red dress and coordinating lipstick. I took pictures with everyone from the church. When I saw Javad walk in, I approached him. "Why, don't you look nice with your burgundy and black," I flirted.

He smiled. "Thank you. You look great, too." I grabbed my pink, Kodak digital camera. "Come on. Let's take a picture," I exclaimed. It was a great shot.

When I got home, I uploaded the pictures. I couldn't stop looking at Javad and me. I tagged him in the picture, and it got a lot of likes and comments. *We do look good together,* I thought to myself, *but I don't want to rush things. Hopefully, we can be great friends.* I couldn't stop blushing as I stared at the picture. Yeah, I had it bad. I knew we were just friends who were obviously attracted to each other.

I felt good about our friendship. We started to hang out more, going to church together, downtown to the park and to bookstores. He was a great guy to hang around; we even invented our own handshake. He was becoming my best friend, but Khadijah told me that he could never replace her, and she was right. One Sunday morning, I logged into my Facebook account and saw a red notification in my inbox. I clicked on it. To my surprise, it was a woman going off about Javad. It was unbelievable. I felt stabbed in the back.

I called Khadijah. "Who is this chick?" Khadijah ranted. "Do I need to jump in my car and roll to ZP?"

I calmed my friend down. "No, I'll figure it out. I just don't know who this woman is. I'm going to talk to him," I explained.

"You better before I mess him up!" she roared.

I chuckled. "Why are you so violent?" I just shook my head.

"You're my best friend; you would do the same for me. Keep me posted."

We hung up our phones, and I sat quietly. *Should I reply to this girl, cut this negro off or let him explain what's going on?* My heart started to race.

I tapped his name on my phone and called him. He answered on the second ring. "Hey," he said happily. "Is everything okay?" he asked.

I paused and exhaled. "A woman inboxed me this morning telling me to leave you alone. I don't know who she is, but you need to clarify to her that we are just friends. Really good friends." He paused. "I'm so sorry, Kendra. She had no right to inbox you," he sighed.

"Who is she to you? Are you dating her?" I asked demandingly.

"She's my ex," he explained. "She saw the picture and got angry. I told her we were just friends —"

I interrupted. "You need to handle this. I'm not for drama. I will have to leave you alone if this will be a problem. Goodbye." I hung up the phone. I was sad. Nonetheless, I had to minister that morning, so I had to be in the right frame of mind and focus. "Just let your will be done, God." I prayed. I calmed my spirit and headed to ZP.

A few months later, everything had calmed down. Javad asked me for forgiveness and told me that everything was handled. My guard was still up, but I gave him another chance. We still spent time together. Our friendship was mending. We decided to become an official couple on March 12, 2011. After much consideration, we chose the Whitfields as the couple who would mentor us. They were the most authentic people we knew.

Our dating relationship was going very well. We had our first kiss in the driveway of my home. He caressed my face and looked me deeply in the eyes. One day, a girl who did not like me in high school decided to spread a vicious rumor about me to a very close friend of his. She proclaimed that I was not who I said I was. She said that I gave my virginity to a guy in the back of the band room at Page High School. It was all malicious lies. Javad's friend told him about it, and he confronted me. Of course, I knew they were lies.

"I know you have known them longer than you have known me. You can believe whatever you feel in your heart to believe," I was done with people. I wasn't accepted anywhere. Thoughts started to run rapidly through my mind. *I can't handle you because you're different? Why do you have standards? You're so weird! Why do you talk like that? Why this? Why that?* I WAS OVERWHELMED! Before I got out of the car, Javad grabbed my hand.

"I believe you, Kendra. I know they want to destroy this relationship." I burst into tears and rested my head on his chest. He wiped my tears away and kissed me on the cheek. People can be so cruel. Despite everything, we continued to date. I met his family in Charlotte. I was terrified to meet his mom, but he told me that I should really be afraid of his father. Ironically, the weather was quite foreboding the day I met his father; the sky boomed with thunder and lightning. However, things turned out alright. I loved his family, and they loved me. Most of my family loved him, too, while some family members merely tolerated him.

Christmas arrived and Javad was acting very weird that morning. "Are you okay?" I asked. "Yeah, babe. I'm fine," he stammered. We prayed and he squeezed my hand. "Let this day be a great day, Lord. Let Your will be done," He smiled, and we drove off to Zion Place.

When we got there, it seemed as if everyone was smiling extra hard. *What's going on?* I wondered. After church, we headed to my big sister Keisha's house. Most of my immediate family were there, including my other sister, Kia, her children, and my parents. Everyone was acting very odd. Even my best friend kept texting me and saying to stay at my sister's house for a little while. She never really gave me an explanation why. Javad and I were going to see his family in Charlotte after we left Keisha's house.

That day, Javad gave me my first gift. It was a Barbie doll with a wedding dress on. My nephew Darius was sitting beside me and kept telling me to look at the dress. But I was so mad, I ignored him. I thought my gift would have been more than a Barbie doll in a wedding dress. What I didn't know was that a second gift was coming. It was a small, red bag with a little black box inside. I opened the black box and to my utter surprise, a diamond engagement ring was in it. My nephews, nieces, and sisters were screaming, while Javad raised his hands to calm everyone down.

"Kendra Anjanette Diggs, will you marry me?"

I dropped my head down, and my eyes filled with tears. Happily, I whispered "Yes. Yes, I will marry you," and I embraced him. I was about to be married — to my best friend!

HIS MASTERPIECE

Chapter 8

I AM HAPPY

I was getting married. I couldn't believe it! Me? Engaged! I felt like I was dreaming, but I still had doubts in my mind. "I don't want to ruin your life," I fretted. "I don't think I'm ready. I barely know how to drive and be on my own. I don't want to be a burden."

Javad held my hand. "You could never be a burden to me. We will work through it. Trust me. I love you," he said as he kissed my hand. I smiled and said. "I love you, too." Despite his attempts to assuage me, there was a lot of doubt in my mind.

As we were preparing for the wedding, I went to go get my yearly checkup to see how I was doing. Earlier in life, I was anemic and pre-diabetic; these were both curable, but if you're not resolute about taking care of your body, they can worsen or manifest in other ways as you age. "You have hypothyroidism, ma'am," my nurse said. Hypothyroidism is an under-active thyroid that doesn't produce enough hormones. It causes a multitude of symptoms within the body.

"So, what do I need to do?" I asked. "It's curable. In order for you not to be on medication, you will have to eat right and exercise," my nurse advised me.

I threw my head back. I hate exercising! But I wanted to live, and I didn't want to be on any medication. I thought of all the people who could hold me accountable. Plus, I had a wedding to get gorgeous for.

Someone popped into my mind — Sabra. She was very fit and disciplined. I knew that she was going to kill me, but I was willing to do what I needed to do. I met up with her after church. I explained the situation to her, and she instantly got on it. "Let's do this!" she yelled enthusiastically.

She made a meal plan for me: no eating after 8, no carbs, no sugar, no red meat or pork. Water was all I could have. We went running early in the morning, and she stayed the course with me. With her, I lost 50 pounds. Javad was doing his own thing as well. We worked out together a few times in the week.

One night, Javad and I were hanging out at his apartment watching a movie. The phone rang. It was Javad's mom. As he listened to her troubled voice, his eyes widened. When she was finished, he hung up the phone.

"Is everything alright?" I questioned. Javad let out a huge breath, "My brother beat his fiancée and now the wedding is off."

I was shocked. His brother Shaquan had gotten engaged around the same time we did. "How could he do such a thing? We need to pray for your brother," I stated. I just didn't understand. How could he do that? My mind flipped back to Javad. *I hope he never puts his hands on me. He's not like his brother. I know he wouldn't do that to me.* Something set off in my spirit, but I ignored it.

Planning our wedding was pretty stressful, so we ended up hiring a wedding planner. She helped us out tremendously. Even my parents did what they could do to help. They just wanted me to be happy. My sister was going through her own challenges, and she needed a favor from my parents. My father asked Javad if he could help my sister out because they had something to do. Javad and I got my parents' car and went to her house. Kia's friends were there, and Javad basically followed me into her room. Thank God, she had clothes on. I didn't even know he was that close behind me. Kia was taking her time and Javad, seemingly irritated, started to jingle the keys. He said, "I have to get the car back to your dad, so you may want to hurry up." I felt like time froze. Everyone was quiet. I knew my sister was about to light into him.

"First of all, don't you come into my house disrespecting me. I can take myself."

Javad replied with a very cocky voice, "But your father asked me to do it." The screaming match began.

I was already stressed out from my day at work, so I pleaded, "Please, don't do this!" They were still screaming, and I said, "Kia, you have to learn to respect him; he's going to be my husband. And the same goes for you too Javad."

Kia sucked her teeth, "I don't need to respect anyone, especially this Negro." With an exasperated breath, I let out, "Well, Kia if you feel that way, you aren't in the wedding anymore."

Next thing you know, a fist flew, and I was down her house steps and in my parents' car. We drove off and met my parents where they were. I told my mother and father what happened. My father was quiet and said, "Okay, we are all going to head back to Kia's house and talk."

Javad and I followed my parents back to Kia's house. She was outside walking back and forth like a tiger in a cage. Javad stayed in his car, but I got out. My dad went up to my sister, and he said, "Kia, you need to stop this right now."

Kia rolled her eyes, "I don't even want to be in the wedding anyway," she exclaimed while still walking back and forth.

With frustration showing on his face, my father responded, "Well, Kia, if you are going to have that attitude, don't be in it!" "No!" said my mother. We are going to get to the bottom of this."

Everything eventually calmed down, and I apologized. "Kia, you know I love you, and I want you in the wedding, but you guys need to learn how to get along. Seriously. We are about to be a family."

Javad got out of the car and hugged her. Kia's face looked like Bishop in the movie "Juice" when he hugged Q after the argument they had. Later on, that night, Kia and I talked on the phone. "I don't trust him, Kendra. He reminds me so much of my ex-fiancé." Her ex was very abusive.

I shook my head, "No, Kia, don't say that! He's nothing like him!" My voice trembled.

"I love you, Kendra. I just want him to treat you right." My sister emphasized.

With confidence, I replied, "And he will." My heart pondered on these things. Why is everyone seeing this but me? He wouldn't harm me intentionally? Right?

HIS MASTERPIECE

Chapter 9

I AM SACRED

August 18, 2012, at 2 p.m. Evangel Fellowship. Our wedding day. It was a bright and sunny day. We went through our premarital counseling, and we believed we were ready. I was extremely nervous and anxious about everything. What if I'm not good enough? I don't think I'm prepared for this. Then the worse thing happened to me, my period came on my wedding day. I tried not to show it on my face, but I was very jittery and upset. Mandisa, my boss from Bovanti, did my makeup; Star did my hair, and Sabra and Tish were my ladies in waiting. My sisters Keisha and Kia were my bridesmaids and my best friend, Khadijah was my maid of honor.

Before the wedding, we exchanged letters. It calmed my fears. *I love you and I need you.* I folded the letter and pulled it close to my heart. It seemed like time went by so quickly. 2 p.m. arrived. I grabbed my father by the arm and inhaled then exhaled.

"Are you ready?" my father asked.

"Yes sir," I replied. The ironic thing is I didn't cry.

I know — out of all the people in the world, *I* didn't cry. Actually, I was relieved that it was almost over. My father and I walked up the aisle to the song, "Wrap Me in Your Arms" by William McDowell. I saw my best friend. He looked so good with his fresh cut and tux. Our eyes met, and we smiled. It was so magical. Javad was crying. My mother and godmother were crying. My nieces were crying. Even my sisters shed a tear or two. It was beautiful.

Pastor O officiated the wedding. Bishop Lockett was supposed to do the blessing, but he was sick. First Lady Lockett did the blessing, and it made me very emotional. Her words soothed my heart. I wish they were both there. But I totally understood.

We kissed for the first time as husband and wife. Now, I was officially married. We were so happy. As we walked back down the aisle, Kia told Javad, "You had better take care of my sister." We both chuckled.

Everything flew by. We took so many pictures that by the end of the ceremony, my face was in pain from smiling. Our reception was held at Triad Christian Center. The evening was great, but it was quite awkward when he went under my dress to get my garter. I covered my face in embarrassment.

Finally, the reception was over. Javad surprised me with a room at the Grandover Hotel, which was very luxurious. That was when I cried. The staff greeted us at the door and everything was laid out perfectly. We went into our room, and we kissed passionately. I was very nervous. I was on birth control, and I made sure it was in my system. We didn't want babies immediately even though we both loved children. It was a night full of passion and romance. We weren't intimate that night, but a few days later everything went as planned. I was afraid, but he calmed my fears. I gave him the gift of my virginity. I knew what sex was, but of course, I wasn't experienced. He was very patient, and he taught me everything he knew.

We went to the beach for our honeymoon. For the first time, I felt free. He was my man and I was his woman. I just felt so secure. After we got back from our honeymoon, we worked as a team. I still had a lot to learn as far as being independent was concerned. It was hard, but he had patience. My heart still pondered though. Is this truly my happily ever after?

HIS MASTERPIECE

Chapter 10

I AM PROTECTED

Months had passed and our relationship grew stagnant and cold. Furthermore, I regained the majority of the weight that I lost prior to getting married. I got too comfortable. The attraction I saw in his eyes when he looked at me gradually disappeared.

"Let's work out together. Maybe that will motivate me," I said optimistically. I had to figure out something to get my husband's love back.

He looked at me and replied, "You will slow me down. You're not as fast as me." He just shook his head as if to say, "it's hopeless." I was frustrated. *I was big before we got married, so why is there an issue now*? I asked myself.

From time to time, we went to the gym together, but he would leave me on the other side all by myself. I was really hurt. *Why is he treating me this way?* I wondered. I saw the love my parents had for each other, and I just wanted my husband to be like my father. I knew their marriage wasn't perfect, but I was sure they loved each other.

Living with Javad was a huge adjustment. I was not used to being on my own, and I really didn't leave and cleave to him as I should have. He didn't like the fact that I went to my parents for a lot of things. If we didn't have the money or anything else, I would just ask, and they gave it to me. He felt like I demeaned him as a man, but from my eyes, that wasn't the case. I just wanted to get things done.

We argued all the time, mainly over stupid stuff. Plus, our methods of handling conflict were miles apart. I wanted to talk and discuss things, but he would leave the apartment. That made me very angry. Our marriage mentors always gave us solid advice, but it would enter one ear and go out the other. We couldn't compromise or even communicate. We blamed each other for each other's faults and never looked at our own. At times, our arguments were so fierce they led to verbal and physical fights. I was spoiled and sheltered, and he was stubborn and unwavering. We were both very insecure individuals. Not a great combination.

One Sunday after church, we argued so badly that I left our apartment and walked in the rain to my sister Keisha's house. I didn't even care. Wet and all. It was very cold outside, and tears were streaming down my face. Next thing you know, I heard a horn beep, and

I turned around. It was one of the elders from my home church. He rolled down his window and said with grave concern, "Girl, what are you doing out here in the rain?"

"I'm just headed to my sister's house," I replied as I dried my face.

He looked around and then asked, "Where is your husband?"
I shook my head. "I don't know." I lied.

"Get in," he said in a calm voice.

I wasn't that far from her house, but he dropped me off. Before I got out of the car, he grabbed my hand and told me, "If you need anything, let me know."

I nodded. "Yes, sir." I shut the car door, quickly ran to my sister's house and knocked on the door. She opened it and looked around. "How did you get here?" she asked, "I walked. I just wanted to hang out with you all today." She looked at me very strangely like she knew I was lying.

"Okay, come in, but take that wet dress off."

I entered, got comfortable and went to sleep. A few hours later, Javad came by and picked me up. When we got home, we went our opposite ways. No affection, no nothing. A few weeks later, my skin started to flare up. I had a bad case of eczema. My skin was so inflamed that it was discolored and flaky. We would get quick remedies, but none ever really worked. I had to go to the doctor, but we simply could not afford it. One night, I had a really bad itching spell. Javad roared, "Can you stop scratching? It's not that serious!"

I cried to him, "Yes, it is. You're not in my body, so you don't know." He didn't comfort me. Instead, he left and slept in the living room. I was devastated. *How could he see me hurting and not comfort me?* I continued to cry and scratched. All of a sudden, my husband bust into our room and threw a glass of cold water on me.

"Shut up! It's not that serious! It's not that serious!" he hollered. Then he jumped on me. I was terrified. I felt the weight of his body getting heavier and heavier on me.

I screamed, "Get off me! You're hurting me!!" I screamed louder. He got up and looked at me through the darkness of our room. I looked at him, numb with fear as he came closer with anger in his eyes. In an instant, his angry eyes became eyes of sadness and regret.

"I'm sorry, baby. I didn't mean to hurt you. Please, forgive me." Then he proceeded to take off my underwear.

I pleaded with him, "Get off me. Get off me!" He tore off my clothes, and I screamed again. I tried to get away from his grip and push him out of the way, but he was too strong. He forced himself on and in me. I couldn't do anything but lay there with tears streaming down my face. There was no sound, except the sound of the bed. I was raped by the man I loved. After he was done, he rolled over and went to sleep. I sat on the edge of the bed, so I wouldn't wake him and started to rock back and forth. "God, help me." I whimpered in the dark room. I was in something I feared — an abusive relationship.

His Masterpiece

Chapter 11

I AM FEARLESS

It was a vicious cycle. Bouts of anger turned into empty apologies. Depression weighed on me heavily. I started to take Benadryl to numb the pain I felt inside. It made me sleep and prevented me from feeling anything. We wore our masks well at church, but outside of the church, we were a mess. A few friends of ours knew what was going on, but other than that, it was our dark secret.

October came, and I had not seen my sister and my mom for a while. I called them, and we decided to go out to eat on October 12. We were sitting at the table when I got a message on Facebook saying, "I'm praying for you and your pastor." Then I kept getting messages saying the same thing. I couldn't figure out what was going on. My phone buzzed again. The text said, "You need to text Pastor O." My heart shuddered. Anxious, I logged onto Facebook on my phone. Dozens of statuses were saying, "Rest in Peace Bishop Lockett."

I instantly lost my appetite. All I could do was grab my head, throw down my phone, and wail.

Something broke in me. My pastor, the man I grew up under all my life, the one who dedicated me to the Lord, the one who was always there for my family when we needed him was gone. My sister and my mom looked at me like I was crazy.

"Kendra, what's wrong?" My mother asked. Her eyes were full of concern.

I looked at her and could barely talk. "Mommy...Bishop Lockett...he's....he's...dead!" I burst into tears again.

My mother gasped and shook her head. My sister Kia began to cry. "No! It can't be true! It can't be true!" my mother shrieked. In disbelief, my mother kept calling Sis. Lockett's phone, then she called Bishop Lockett's phone hoping it was not true.

We paid for our food and left. I was numb for the rest of the day. They called for a mass meeting at our church, so we went to church that evening. Sis Lockett walked in with Faith, Pastor Josh, Pastor O, and James, Faith's husband; their faces were full of grief, I couldn't do anything but cry. They were so strong even though they were in pain. That evening, Javad met me at the church. Grief has a way of bringing people together. We hugged each other and held hands, which we hadn't done in a while.

After we left the church, we went home. It was a quiet evening as we lay in each other's arms. "I know we have our issues, but we need to be there for Pastor O. He needs us," I said with my eyes full of tears.

Javad nodded his head. "You're right. We do need to be."

Bishop Lockett's homecoming celebration lasted two days. Seeing him in the casket was heart-wrenching. I knew he was in heaven, but I wanted him back here. I didn't get a chance to say goodbye, and I missed him very much. Why did God take him? I was grief-stricken, but I knew he would rather be in heaven than on Earth. I remembered one of his famous quotes, "You may miss me when I'm gone, but don't miss my God." Those words comforted my broken heart. We sang his song at his gravesite.

> There's a wave of your glory,
> That angels run into,
> There's a wave of your glory,
> That angels run into,
> When He's exalted.

When we drove away from the gravesite, more tears flowed from my eyes. I said in my heart, *I'm going to make him proud of me.* But most importantly, *I'm going to make the God we serve proud of me as well.*

A few months later, I decided I wanted to go to beauty school in January. I was tired of my job at Bovanti. I wanted to grow outside of that job. Plus, I felt it was time for me to accomplish my dream to be a

MAC Girl. I believed if I had my cosmetology license and MAC under my belt I could do anything. Javad knew I was unhappy and wanted to quit, I ended up making a hasty, irresponsible decision to quit Bovanti without a solid plan. It was a risk, but I wanted to go to school. Javad was the main source of income for our home. However, when I didn't have a job, I freelanced for myself. I did a lot of makeup for clients.

In spite of our challenges, the one thing Javad and I could do right was hustle and make money. I did makeup, last extensions, and brows.

We used social media at our advantage and posted on Craigslist every day. I enrolled at Empire Beauty School. Javad made decent money with his job even though I could tell he hated it. Nevertheless, we had to do what we had to do. My parents knew we needed help, so they would assist as much as they could. But as I said earlier, Javad detested that. One day, we got into an argument over all sorts of things. We yelled and screamed at each other. Unexpectedly, a loud scream bellowed from his belly, and he spat a large glob of spit on my face. Stunned, I didn't say anything.

It was as quiet as the grave on our way home. A big shade of tension covered us. He dropped me off at the apartment and drove away. I didn't see him until later that evening. *Who is this man I married? Is love supposed to be this hard? Isn't he supposed to be my best friend?* Our marriage vows said for better or for worse; we seemed to be worse! What could I do?

HIS MASTERPIECE

Chapter 12

I AM CAPABLE

I started beauty school that January and was truly excited! I was one step closer to my dream of being a MAC Girl. While I was in school, I was a housewife, went to school full-time, and did a lot of freelance work for myself. But in my mind, it still wasn't enough. I wanted to go to counseling a bit more. So, my best friend recommended we see a couple at her church: the Steins. They were perfect for us, but Javad didn't care for them. I was irritated. It was as if no one could reason with him. It was his way or no way.

School was my escape from my problems at home at times. I was the weirdo in my class. As usual, I'm the one who is different. I made some great friends and associates though. Once I was on the salon floor, I had great clients. Ms. Cammy was my favorite client; I loved her. She was a former MAC artist, and she always encouraged me to keep going after my dreams; she also showed me everything she knew and sold her full MAC Kit to me, which was a blessing. During this time, I wore weave – a lot. I loved to support my fellow classmates and their credit. Plus, my husband loved hair. I had to keep him happy. One day, I decided to get a relaxer and a sew in at the same time. My hair was fly, but when it was time to take it out, it was damaged and breaking bad. A classmate advised me to cut it off, which was very dramatic for me, but in a strange way, I liked it. However, when Javad saw my hair, he was not pleased. Actually, he hated it. I had to start wearing wigs immediately.

One morning before I went to school, I was sitting on the bed. He had agreed to take me to school in the morning, instead of me catching the bus. Our counselors advised that because it didn't look good that I had to catch the bus when a car was available. We got into an argument about our finances, our counselors, everything. It was another screaming match. Next thing you know, Javad grabbed me, shook me, and then threw me against the wall. My makeup and brushes flew everywhere. He went to the living room, took his belongings, and headed outside to the car. Petrified, I went to the bathroom and looked in the mirror. My lip was swollen. Again. I remained quiet. I proceeded to get into the car. It was silent, no music, only the sound of the engine going.

When he dropped me off, I went into the school and barely spoke. I didn't want anyone to notice my lip, but I think everyone did. It all hit the fan when my father came to see me for his haircut. After his service was done, we went outside and talked. I collapsed in his arms and cried. He looked at me and saw my swollen lip.

"Dad, I'm so sorry. I'm sorry you had to see me this way," I stammered.

He simply looked at me and said, "Kendra, it's up to you; you have to make a decision to leave. Your mother and I are here for you." He hugged me again, got into his car and drove off. A few hours later, my mother called and gave me an ear full. "You are leaving him! I don't care what you say!" she shouted. "I know this is your husband, but he is acting like a fool, a complete fool."

I tried to reason with my mom. "I know Javad and I have issues, but I love him. Not only does he need to change, I do too." My mother didn't want to hear it. "You're leaving him as I said!"

After I got home from school, my mother and sisters were at my apartment ready to help me with my things. I moved back with my parents. I was ashamed. This was the first time we had separated. Moreover, I knew other people were against us getting married in the first place, and I didn't want them to win. I wanted to be back with my husband. I didn't care that we had issues, and I didn't want to be divorced. *I'm going to get my marriage back.* I said to myself. *No one is going to say I am the first divorced woman of my family or my church family. I refuse to let it happen!*

HIS MASTERPIECE

Chapter 13

I AM RESILIENT

Graduation was upon me. I only had a few more credits left until I was out of school. Javad and I were still separated, but we continued to communicate. After I officially graduated beauty school, we got back together. We tried to work through our differences, but it was still a struggle. I decided to pursue MAC again. Luckily, they were hiring. I was so excited. I was one step closer to my dream job. I had a burning passion to perfect my artistry and be the best because, in my opinion, MAC was the best. After two interviews, out of the five girls who wanted a position with MAC, only two girls were chosen. I was one of the two. Even though it was just a freelance position, it was a foot in the door, and I was very grateful.

My relationship with my husband was getting a bit better day by day. We still went to our counselors every now and then. One evening, Javad shared his heart with me. He wanted to be an entrepreneur. I was very skeptical. "I don't know Jay. I don't think this is the best idea right now." I was worried. "That's a huge risk, and we barely get along now."

Javad held my hand and said, "Kendra, this is what I want to do. I want to be an entrepreneur. I just need your support. You had my support when you decided to go to beauty school. Let me do this. I can do this. Let me lead you. Trust me," he insisted.

I really didn't trust him or his idea, but I went along with it anyway.

Eventually, the idea of moving away came up. "Leave?" I gasped as my eyes widened. "I would be away from my family, friends, and from Zion Place. I mean, I would love to move there eventually, but don't you think this is pretty drastic?"

Javad disagreed. "No, we need a fresh start and move. I have a plan. Trust me."

When Javad had his mind on something, he was persistent and would do anything to make it happen.

One day, I truly thought about his suggestion. I didn't have any freelance hours in Greensboro with MAC, so I would probably have more opportunities in another city to be a makeup artist and work for myself. That thought excited me more than anything else.

"We just can't up and leave. We need to talk to our families, friends, and Pastor O," I insisted. He literally wrote out a plan for us to abide by. We discussed it with my parents first.

My mother and my sisters were totally against it. "Out of the question! How dare he try to take you away from us? I really don't like him!" Mom fussed.

"Mom, it would be a better opportunity for me. Plus, Javad and I can start all over again. Everyone here knows our business."

"Not everyone!" she yelled with tears in her eyes. "I don't agree with this. I don't agree with this at all!"

I looked at my mom. She was very upset. "Mommy, please, trust me. I'm grown now, and I have to start making decisions on my own. Let me do this. I will survive. Let me grow up and be with my husband."

My mother sighed and hugged me. I wasn't a little girl anymore. I had to put my big girl panties on and face responsibility.

We made our preparations to leave. Javad and I hustled hard for the extra money. We sold our furniture. I did makeup, and he hustled his business. A month before leaving Greensboro, I had to meet with a client at Panera Bread. Javad had somewhere to go as well, but we ended up arguing again. "You are acting just like your brother. Just mean and cruel." I fumed boldly. Javad hated to be compared to anyone, especially his brother who was truly not a definition of a man in his mind.

His eyes filled with rage, a face I had never seen before came on him. "How dare you compare me to him?" He screamed.

We started to fight in the bathroom, and his nail dug deep into my chest as he threw me into the shower. I got up with tears in my eyes, and I tasted blood.

"I'm sorry. Please, stop!" I pleaded. We were fighting until we got into our bedroom.

"I'm my brother, you said?" Javad sneered and threw me into the wall, which left a huge hole. I fell, and he kicked me in my shins.

"Please, stop! I'm sorry, Please, forgive me." I cried as my weak body lay on the floor.

He stopped and looked at me with disgust then gathered his things and left. My shoulder and legs were throbbing in pain. I could barely get up. But I had to go to my meeting with my client. I had to get ready. I cleaned up what we messed up, fixed my face, reapplied my makeup, put some new clothes on and walked to Panera Bread. Javad wasn't there, and I didn't want my family to see me. It was a 20-minute walk, but I didn't care. I had my headphones on, but I didn't hear any music. My ears were ringing and the piercing thoughts took over my mind. I repeated the events that had just happened in my head. I couldn't believe someone I loved would treat me this way. I must've deserved it.

When I arrived at Panera Bread, I sat down at the table and waited for my client. She walked in, and I put on my fake smile. We sat and talked for an hour. My shoulders and my legs were on fire, but you would never have known. After a good meeting, I sat quietly for another hour or so. My ears started to ring again as I stared into a blank space. *Maybe I should kill myself. It would get me out of my misery.* With my eyes blurry from my tears, I looked outside, and it was night time. I got up and walked back home.

When I got home, I took off my clothes, got comfortable, took some pain medicine, and got an ice pack from the fridge. I saw the scar on my chest and the dried blood. So, I got some hydrogen peroxide and cleaned it up some more. Sore and hurt, laid down on our bed.

A few hours later, Javad came back home. He brought some food with him. He came next to me and once again apologized with tears in his eyes.

"Kendra, please forgive me. I'm so sorry. I won't do it again. I know we have our issues, but I need you and I love you."

He proceeded to stand me up. He fell on his knees and held my waist. "Please forgive me," he pleaded as he cried.

My ears were still ringing, I was still in a daze as he held me. As he was talking, I still couldn't hear the words, but I saw his mouth move. I heard the tempter's voice say, "Take his life and yours. You won't have to deal with him or yourself anymore. Why go through this? Do it!" Then the voice left me. That shook me to the core.

I looked into his eyes blankly and saw a stranger. I saw a man who was supposed to love, protect, and be there for me, but instead bullied and beat me into submission. Being with him was a nightmare, but I could forgive him again, right? I breathed in and exhaled.

"I forgive you, and I love you, too," I said.

He stood up, hugged me, and kissed me. Then, he laid me back down and started to rub my shoulder. Afterward, he laid down beside me. "We are going to be okay," Javad reassured me.

I nodded my head. "I know."

It was quiet for the rest of the evening. When he fell asleep, I got up and looked out the window. Our windowsill had an alarm on it. It was 2 a.m. I walked into the bathroom and looked at myself in the mirror. I looked at my face with heavy bags under my eyes, the scar on my chest, and my bruised shoulder. I didn't see me. I didn't see beauty. I didn't see virtue. I saw a failure. I sat on the bathroom mat, and I grabbed my head. I began to wail and cry. "There has to be more to life than this." I said to myself. "I want to be free."

The time had come. It was time for us to move. It was a Sunday. We had enough money saved up, but to be honest, it was a very irresponsible move. Still, I followed my husband.

"We are one step closer to our dreams," Javad smiled. "We can start all over again. We will be able to breathe."

I smiled back. I wondered what this city had in store for us.

HIS MASTERPIECE

Chapter 14

I AM CAPABLE

New city. New opportunities. New adventures. Javad and I were truly excited. We were getting along a bit better. We even made a video talking about what we went through in our marriage. We felt led to do it. It was our testimony.

Some people applauded our boldness, while others were angry. We just decided to be transparent even though I knew people would view us differently. We joined Elevation Church because we heard so many great things about Pastor Furtick's ministry. We ended up joining a small group.

We agreed to stay with his mom and family for a little while and had our own room. Javad worked on his blogging business, and I worked on my freelance makeup business.

Before we left, I talked to JT who was the manager at MAC in Greensboro at that time about getting some freelance hours. He agreed that they had more hours at their counter. He gave me all of the managers' contact information and wished me the best. I called all the counters and luckily, I got a response from Caroline Bradley.

Being around this team automatically made me feel as if they were family. I loved the team there. However, I desperately wanted to be a permanent artist, so I hustled my behind off to make a good impression on her and the regional manager. I attracted a lot of clients, and they took notice of that.

When the freelance hours were cut, I had to figure out what to do. Money was pretty tight and there were a lot of things Javad and I didn't have, but we did the best we could. I actually hooked up with a girl named Leila and started doing makeup with her at a leased booth from her shop. That's when I got to know a lot of my makeup artist friends. We met at a makeup workshop, and we automatically connected. To rent a booth, I had to give Leila a deposit. Javad and I barely had any money, but I knew in my heart I could do this makeup bar. I ended up pawning my wedding ring. I was so devastated that I actually cried.

"I'll be able to buy you a new one," Javad said as he kissed me on the cheek.

I was sad, but I knew with the makeup bar I would get clients often. God was definitely looking out for me because I always had clients. I was grateful.

Things were getting better between us, but one day, I was on his computer doing some research for my makeup business. I hit the history tab and was shocked at what I saw. I guess he forgot to clear the browsing data. What I saw hurt my heart. Porn sites. Nothing but porn sites. I confronted him dead on, "Are you watching porn?" I asked with tears in my eyes. "Am I not enough for you?"

I was already very insecure about my weight and my body. It was bad enough that he had already told me that I was proportioned incorrectly; I was stiff. He felt like he was married to an old woman. I gained a lot of my weight back and more. At that time, I had an Afro, and I felt as if he wasn't attracted to me anymore. I tried to lose weight and eat right, but it just didn't work.

"I do everything you want me to do, but you're still not satisfied?!" I ranted.

"I apologize Kendra; these women mean nothing to me," he said.

His brother overheard our conversation and told me, "You never know Kendra; you might learn something."

I thought about it, I pondered on what I was taught about pornography. It distorts the mind. It allows you to have this perspective of what sex is, but it's not real. In spite of that, I wanted my husband to be happy, so I finally decided to be open to it.

My birthday was coming up in June, so Javad and I decided to save some money to get my hair done. At least, with some hair on my head, he would pay attention to me. A woman named Cassandra fixed my hair, and when I tell you I was gone with the wind fabulous, you couldn't tell me anything.

I felt like myself again. Sure enough, as soon as I got the hair, Javad could not keep his hands off me or stop taking pictures. We decided one afternoon we were going to watch a video. My heart was racing. I had never done that before. What does a church girl know about porn? Absolutely nothing!

There was no one in the house but us. Javad locked our door. We pulled a video up on his phone. My eyes widened and the adrenaline ran through my body. It was like a drug. Then a feeling of release came over me. My husband told me what to do to myself and to him. It was a great feeling. But then, I started to feel guilty. He did too — well, sorta.

"Are you okay?" he asked.

I just nodded. I knew it was wrong, but it felt so right. As long as my husband was happy, that's all that mattered. I told myself, *I gotta start looking like these women on these videos. Maybe he would love me more.* But then I pondered, *is his happiness worth more than mine?*

HIS MASTERPIECE

Chapter 15

I AM WELL

Things started to go downhill. Lots of crazy things were going on with his mom's finances. When she asked Javad to do something that would get him in trouble, he refused. Hence, we got kicked out of the house. He really didn't have a great relationship with his mother's side of the family, but he had a great one with his dad's side.

We had to move again. This time, we relocated to a small city. We didn't have stable incomes, so we continued to struggle financially. Nonetheless, it was a beautiful home on a steep hill. But it was a house full of people: his two brothers, sister-in-law, niece, dad, stepmom, and us. We slept on the couch. We had good times there, but the bad times seemed to outweigh the good.

Eventually, Javad got two jobs. Since there were no hours at MAC, I had to find a job too. I still freelanced, but there were not as many opportunities then as they were at the beginning of the year. I got a kiosk job working for another cosmetic company, but that was for a limited time. I couldn't make it to work as frequently as I should, so I was let go. Javad was furious, and of course, he blamed me. We argued and fought.

One night we argued very badly in his car. He said nasty things just to provoke me. I was so mad I fought him while he was driving. The funny thing is he didn't fight me back this time. He allowed me to smack him and scratch him. He just sat there. I think he did it to make the point that he wasn't the only one who had issues in our relationship.

His father refused to let us have unnecessary drama in his house. He promised if we fought in his house, he would gather up our things and tell us to leave. I was just an emotional wreck. I was a drama queen. I had a fit that we couldn't do anything for our wedding anniversary even though I knew there was no extra money in the house. However, he surprised me.

He took me out with some money his brother gave him because his brother knew how unhappy we were. It seemed like we attracted chaos everywhere we went. On top of that, he had been watching porn again. I was very upset, but my flesh started to weaken. I started to watch it with him, but more troubling than that was I began to watch it by myself without him knowing. It was addictive. I loved the sensation I got, the adrenaline rush. I was addicted and didn't even realize it. It was my little dirty secret.

A few months later, we had another ordeal. Our car broke down. My husband hated to depend on anyone, and we really needed a car. We went to a small car dealership and thankfully, we were approved.

At this point, my skin started to flare up really badly again. I had broken out all over my body. On top of that, I had to take the weave out of my hair, which made him upset.

"Why did you take out your hair? You know I hate natural hair!" he fussed.

"Well, I'm sorry, but you know I couldn't keep it on that long. My hair needs a break," I threw my head back. "I'll just ask my mom and dad to help me with some hair," I sighed.

"No!" Javad blurted out, "You're always running back to your mom and dad, demeaning me as a man."

I shook my head in frustration. "Well, if you started to act like one, I wouldn't have to call them." It got quiet. You could hear a pin drop.

"I'm about to send you back to Greensboro. You can be replaced," he sassed me.

I turned around and looked at him. "Oh, I can be replaced? Well, fine, send me back. As a matter of fact, I'll help you!" I screamed back.

He was tired and so was I. I thought about a friend of mine, Jaclyn Michaels. She used to attend the Evangel Fellowship. From time to time, Javad and I would hang out with her and her husband. They were entrepreneurs. They even gave us money one time for no reason.

It was a blessing to have them in our lives. She told me if I ever needed anything don't ever hesitate to call her. "I'm a phone call away," she would say.

Later on, that night after we argued, he was sleeping on the couch. I went into the bathroom and called her. It was 11:30. She answered the phone, and I burst into tears. I cried, "Please come and get me. I'm done. I'm ready to go."

Without hesitation, she told me to pack my stuff. "We are on our way," she said.

I packed up what I could and sneaked out of the house. I literally walked all the way to the top of the hill to get to their car. We drove off in the middle of the night.

When I got to their house, I was finally at peace. I did not feel that peaceful in a very long time. I cried myself to sleep knowing something was about to happen. I felt it in my bones.

His Masterpiece

Chapter 16

I AM STRONG

My phone rang off the hook. We were supposed to pick up the car, but I wasn't there. Of course. He needed my signature. I refused. I finally answered him.

"Javad, I need to stay away from you for a while. You need some time to yourself." "Kendra, I really need your signature," he shouted over the phone. "I can be replaced remember? Get my replacement to do it." Then I hung up.

Javad eventually got kicked out his father's house, and I had to go back there to get my stuff. As usual, Javad had to have the final word. He looked at me and said, "If it wasn't for you and you b***h emotions, we wouldn't be getting kicked out."

I looked at him and said, "Well, I left. You are getting kicked out. That's why I'm staying away from you to get my b***h emotions together."

After all my stuff was packed, I left with Jaclyn and her family. A few months went by and I was still staying with them. I was a bit of a loner and spent much of my time in my room, which was pretty rude, but it was peaceful. Jaclyn helped me get my hair done and find some relief for my skin.

I was grateful to have this family in my life. Eventually, MAC hired me as a permanent artist. It was 15 hours a week, but I didn't care. I was official. I did what I had to do for the job I loved. I took Uber, Lyft, and at times, Jaclyn and her husband would take me to work. It was crazy getting back and forth, but I didn't care. I loved my job that much.

I started to miss Javad, and eventually, we got back together again. He promised that this time would be different. We went to church more often and got counseling. I moved away from Jaclyn's house and went to live with Javad at his friend Joey's house. We made an agreement to rent the room and pay our rent on time. My thyroid issues were getting under control, and my skin was healing rapidly. We were happy again; we communicated more, laughed more, and it seemed like everything was fine. But once again, things started to change.

I have to admit, I became very lazy. I would cook sometimes and do partial cleaning from time to time. I was just very slothful and didn't care. Having hypothyroidism does have an effect on your body and taking the medicine did help. However, some of the side effects can make you crazy if you don't know how to handle them. I was still trying to eat right but was never successful. Javad would leave the house after he got off work and never told me where he was going. Eventually, he told me he was visiting another couple whom we both knew. Apparently, all of his brothers and other friends were there as well. They all just smoked cigarettes or weed, drank, watched movies or played games like Charades. He invited me to join them, but I was very uncomfortable — at first. I just wanted to be around my husband, but I guess I was a headache to be around. That's why he would leave for hours and not come back until early the next morning. I was a burden. That was my perspective.

One day, I got bold and hid his car keys. I just wanted him to spend time with me. I told him how much I missed him, but he had his mind on other things. He changed the password on his computer, his emails, and phone.

"Are you cheating on me?" I questioned him with seriousness on my face. He nodded his head. "No!" he replied quickly. I looked at him and asked, "How come you don't want to be around me?"

He took his jacket. I jumped on his back and grabbed the keys. We began to wrestle. He's stronger, so you know he won. He snatched his keys and left. I was in the house alone. I kept calling Javad, but he got my service cut off. I couldn't call or talk to anyone.

Joey came home, and I asked him if he could run me to the store. Whenever I felt bad, I would turn to eating or take Benadryl. This time, I bought a bottle of wine and two pints of ice-cream. I cried while eating the ice-cream and drank a whole bottle of wine by myself, straight to the head. It burned my chest. I didn't even know what type of wine I bought. It was the first time I had ever gotten drunk, and I felt nauseous.

I didn't see my husband until the next afternoon. Neither of us spoke a word. Reeking of weed, he came into the room, jumped in the shower, and went to work. Later that night when he got off work, he took yet another shower, got dressed, and left again. I was so lonely. This went on for weeks. Eventually, he invited me to his friend's home. Desperate to fit in, I took shots and drank beer. I did not want my husband to feel like I was judging him in this environment since I would typically ridicule him for similar behavior. It was a turn off to me, but that never seemed to deter him from doing it.

One night, I simply couldn't stomach the thought of going back there. I begged him not to go. Unaffected, he put on his jacket and took his keys.

"I'm going with you," I insisted as I grabbed my things.

Javad pushed me back into the house. "No, you're not!" he exclaimed as he left me in the doorway.

I ran through the front door and chased him up the street. He got into the car, stared at me, and drove off. I was so desperate, I chased after the car. To this day, I don't know why I thought I could catch up with him, but at that moment, I would have done anything for him not to leave me alone once more. I walked back to the house and, thankfully, he didn't disconnect the service to my phone again. I called my mom and filled her in on what had transpired. My father took the phone, and his parting words to me were harsh but true: "Kendra, don't call here anymore worrying your mother. You made the choice to stay with this man, but it is still your choice to stay or leave. You are a grown woman. You have to make this decision, not your mother or me. Have a good night!" Then he hung up the phone. My father never really talked to me like that. I suppose he was fed up. Why complain about a situation you choose to be in?

I had a one-on-one with my manager, Caroline. I could not hold the turmoil inside anymore, so I broke down and told her everything that was happening to me. She handed me some tissue. "Everything is going to be okay." She smiled. "If you need anything, please, let me know." She gave me the biggest hug. I really needed that hug. I truly loved my MAC family. But my heart was still heavy. There was a void that I couldn't fill. How did my life turn out this way?

HIS MASTERPIECE

Chapter 17

I AM ENOUGH

Spring was in the air. My niece was begging me to come back home to do her makeup for her birthday. I could not say no. A few weeks before my niece's birthday, Javad and I started arguing about finances on our way home after a long day at work.

Even though we were yelling at each other, I still wanted to spend time with him. He refused and told me no. I stayed in the car. He unbuckled my seatbelt, and I buckled it back.

"I'm not leaving," I snapped. "This is my car, too! I'm coming with you!"

He shouted, "No, Kendra, you are not!"

He pulled me from the car and knocked my purse over, spilling its contents onto the street. I screamed and told him I was not going anywhere. We were fighting in front of the house, and I was screaming and crying as he dragged me to the porch. I sat there as he got into the car and pulled off. All I could do was try to recover the items that were on the street.

After I regained my composure, I cleaned my face, took a shower, and got ready for bed. I figured if I wasn't going anywhere, I might as well put on my pajamas and sleep. I heard the keys jingle at the door. It was Joey's mother. I had to tell her what happened in front of her house and apologize.

"I am sorry for our behavior. It won't happen again." I explained to her what caused the ruckus. She nodded her head.

"All is forgiven," she replied. "But you guys need to learn how to get along with each other or separate."
I agreed. Then I went to our room and fell asleep.

A month later, my niece's birthday was approaching. It was time for me to go back to Greensboro. I had to do my niece's makeup for her birthday dinner.

My sisters, Keisha and Kia, picked me up. In retrospect, I think that was intentional, so they would run into my husband. Thankfully, he wasn't home. I packed up what few belongings I had, but I left my wedding dress.

"I hope he hasn't done anything else," said Kia.

"No, we have our issues, but we're fine," I insisted.

Kia rolled her eyes. She knew I was lying, but she didn't press the issue.

Finally, I was back at home with my family. It was good to be around people who really loved me. Dacia was ready to get her face beat. I was excited; my oldest niece was growing up in front of my eyes. After her birthday party, we all went to my parents' house, relaxed and caught up with each other's lives.

After being in Greensboro for a few days, I got a call that turned my world upside down. Javad sighed on the other side of the phone, "Kendra, this isn't going to work anymore. You are not welcome back at Joey's house." I scrunched my face and held my tears.

"Says who?" I questioned.

"His mother. She said the atmosphere of the house changed since you left."

A dagger pierced my heart. *Geez, was I that bad to be around? This is ridiculous!*

"We tried, Kendra, but it just didn't work. Goodbye." He hung up.

I paced back and forth. When I tried to call him back, my phone didn't have service because he had removed me from the account. *What am I going to do? She kicked me out, not my husband? My job is down there. How am I going to survive? Will I have to give up my job at MAC?*

My mother and sisters were furious. "Oh, I can't stand him!" my sister Keisha blurted out. My best friend Khadijah came to the house. She knew everything that was going on and was concerned about my job. I called my manager from my mother's phone and told her what happened. She was angry and told me to keep her posted on any progress. I called all the women's shelters looking for a place to stay. That upset my mother.

"You are *not* staying in a shelter!"

"I don't have any other choice, Mom. I'll do what I can do."

My mind then went to Cassandra, the lady who styled my hair. I called her immediately and explained what had transpired. Initially, she was quiet. After a few moments, she welcomed me into her home. I was so relieved. I called my manager and told her that I found a place to stay.

She was very happy, and she gave me another day off, so I could settle in and get my things together. My mother and father brought me back to the city.

Cassandra's house was beautiful. She had three girls, and they were a blast to be around. I did what I had to do to keep my mind focused and maximize at my job. I couldn't focus on my issues with my husband. Some of my coworkers knew I was going through something, but the only people who knew the heavy details were Amelia and Caroline. Amelia Tilford was like a big sister to me.

She had big, blue eyes and beautiful blond hair. I could talk to her about life, and she would listen. She always said I deserved better. One of my makeup artist friends Brianna and I got close too. She was the same girl I worked with at the makeup bar. She would help me out with rides and just be a listening ear.

I still took Ubers, Lyfts, buses, and rides to get back and forth. Eventually, I got tired. I stopped going to church completely. I missed Javad. I was depressed. I took Benadryl to make me relax and numb the pain. My dark secret still haunted me. I was addicted to porn and masturbation.

I just needed the release and ironically, since my husband wasn't there, I would moan his name. I didn't like the woman I was becoming. I was so stressed out. My hair was falling out, and my throat was always on fire. I didn't have enough money to do anything. Javad wanted to get back together again, but I refused.

"I don't want to be a burden anymore. Just let me be by myself."

He did everything to try to get my attention. He even inboxed me a suicide note on Facebook. If I didn't leave, who knows what would have happened? He could've harmed me or worse. I just didn't trust him. All of my family members and friends called and texted me regularly telling me I just needed to come home. I gave in.

I hoped I could transfer my job back to Greensboro, so I talked to Amelia about it the following week. She put in a good word for me with her best friend, JaNelle McBride who was the manager at the counter in Greensboro. It was 6 months since I was employed, so the transfer would have been easy.

I went home, and I said a quick prayer, "God I know You and I are not on the best terms right now, but You know what's going on. Please, make a way for me to go back home." A few hours later, I received a text from Amelia saying, "Somebody is looking out for you in the sky because they have three positions opened."

I cried. God still loved me despite everything. The interview process went smoothly. I got a call back a few days later. I was hired. I had a job and I was going home. Of course, I was going to miss being around my old MAC family.

I returned home before my birthday. I didn't let Javad know because I knew it would be messy. I just wanted to be with my family and friends. I simply wanted to find true love.

HIS MASTERPIECE

Chapter 18

I AM UNSHAKABLE

Being back in Greensboro was bittersweet. I was happy to be back at home with family, but I was embarrassed and ashamed that I had to prove the people who were against my marriage right. I didn't talk to many people, especially at my church. I was paranoid. I felt that they were not genuinely concerned about me. They were just being nosy. I was very guarded. I stayed with my sister Kia and her family.

It's always hard to stay with family members, especially siblings. but I didn't have any other choice. I was bitter, lonely, and had a lot of unforgiveness in my heart. I was angry at my church. I felt like no one was there for me. Empty words of "I'm praying for you" or "I'm here for you" didn't resound in my spirit. They were nothing but words. I really didn't believe anyone was genuine.

Javad and I had our last altercation over the phone. Apparently, he had been drinking, and he just called to start an argument. My sister grabbed the phone, and they started to yell at each other. He threatened to kill her and me. I blocked him after that and stopped all communication. I started to invest in weave again, but something in me said, *this is not you*. I wore weaves all of my life, but something just didn't feel right this time.

So, I decided to cut all my hair off again. I cut it into a cute hairstyle. I decided to try to have a male friend, but that didn't work out too well. My husband had a fit, inboxed him and cursed him out. There was no chance of me having a guy friend. Yet, he took pictures with women all the time, especially in strip clubs.

In North Carolina, you have to be separated for a year in order for your divorce to be final. I just wanted it to be over. I didn't want to go to court or anything. No alimony. No support. No nothing. I just wanted it to go away. I just wanted to go on with my life, and I wanted him to go on with his. On Sundays, I would just sit in church and everything would go in one ear and out the other. I stopped singing completely. I didn't realize how powerful the gift of song was. In fact, it was the key to my deliverance. I didn't see myself as worthy. I did go up to the altar one day and rededicate my life, but it didn't stick. I was still struggling. Every day, I continued to struggle with porn and masturbation. I still took Benadryl to ease the torment that I felt. I was looking for love in all the wrong places and longed for affirmation. I attracted all the wrong attention to myself, especially when it came to men. I downloaded apps like Tinder, Go Fish, and even guys on Facebook who just added me I gave my attention and time to. I was desperate to find love and fill the void of loneliness.

Every guy who was attracted to me just wanted one thing. Men sense when a woman is vulnerable. I was even enticed by lesbianism. I saw so many successful relationships or what I believed to be successful, and I craved that love from anyone. When I went to work, I knew how to act the part. On social media, I would take all the selfies, so I could attract "love" my way. However, when I left work, my countenance was down. I tried to be someone I wasn't. I wore fake nose rings just to impress people and hid behind my career as a makeup artist. But I was tired, lonely, and sad.

One night, in my room as I was taking my Benadryl and crying myself to sleep, I heard a voice clear as day, "I'm going to take your voice and your life." At that point, I was ready to give up and die. I didn't want to live. I was ashamed. I cried out and screamed in the pillow: "I'm tired. I'm tired of being this way. Just take my life!" I was ready to get out of here.

April 15, 2016, I had an encounter with the living God, just God and me. I was humbled In His presence. The holy, loving God was still fond of me. That was amazing! He showed me myself. He revealed many things that I didn't want to face. I had to take responsibility for my life. I had to forgive and release many people, including my ex-husband and me.

"Your identity is in Me, My daughter. Don't try to be anything you are not. Dwell in Me, and I will dwell in you. I made you. You are My masterpiece." I had never felt the love of God so strong. I had been in church all my life but never experienced that before. My heart overflowed with love. Jesus loves me. I was forgiven of everything and every sin I had ever committed.

That Sunday, we had to share our testimonies. I gave my testimony in front of the church. Suddenly, I felt at peace and an overwhelming presence came over me. "Sing to me," a still small voice said. So I started singing as if there was no one there. It was an audience of one: my heavenly Father. I just cried all over again. There's nothing like being free in God. After I went home, I couldn't stop smiling. I looked at myself in the mirror. I wasn't the same woman. That following Monday, I got a letter. My divorce was finalized on the 15th. The same day I had an encounter with God. I knew it was finally over, and I had to move on with my life.

I joined AWOL Fitness, and I did the 90-Day challenge with my homegirl Chloe. She had joined months before me, and she looked amazing. "You can do this!" she encouraged me. "As a matter of fact, I'll pick you up." We started together and the days she couldn't go, I caught the bus. I was ready to make a change, not only spiritually but physically as well. I eventually moved out of my sister's house and moved to another house. The house was closer to the gym so it made it better for me to just jump on the bus and head downtown. When I started to catch the 5:30 a.m. bus, I would get to the depot by 6:00 a.m.

Eventually, I ended up training under another gentleman, Roland Ralston. He was very intimidating, and he knew it. I was scared of him. Those big eyes and muscles were scary! I was on my vegan journey, but he told me I wasn't vegan anymore. I gave him the strangest look. "Just follow what I say and you'll get the results you want." I cocked my head to the side and hoped he was right. He took me grocery shopping because he knew I didn't have a car. I don't think he realized how much that touched me. I was mad though because he dictated everything I couldn't eat. I was a little angry but I got over it. After we went shopping, we had small talk.

"What are your dreams? What are your goals?" he asked me.

"I don't know, I'm just trying to make it to next week." I chuckled but he was dead serious. I stopped chuckling.

He promised me, "Well, if you stick with me, you'll be successful."

My guard came down. What was the worst that could happen? I was 245 pounds when I left Charlotte, then I slowly began to lose weight. I was 210 pounds. But being under Roland, I lost 30 pounds. In total, I lost 67 pounds on my weight loss journey. I ran a 5K and went hiking up the mountains, which I would never do again. He challenged me to think outside the box, be the best Kendra I can be and also be determined to be in the best shape that I can be in. I truly realized my body didn't belong to me.

Even though I slackened up and gained weight again because life happened to me, I'm determined to be healthy, physically, and spiritually.

I still desired that intimate relationship with someone and I got distracted with men who I had no business being with at all. Even the desire for porn became stronger, but I had to fight it in order to experience true love and intimacy, which began with God, I have to be like Jesus, and be holy as He is holy. I must know the difference between men or even people who value me from those who just desire me. Is it a struggle sometimes? Yes, however, even though I'm human, my desire to make God happy with my life is stronger.

Although I am single again, I am not lonely. I even lost my closest friends on the journey of finding myself. When God has a greater plan and purpose for your life, people who you thought would be there for a lifetime, disappear. I was sad, but God was right there. God is my husband, best friend, strength, joy, the air I breathe, my everything. If God wants to release me to be married again, that's great, but if not, that's fine too. I'm determined to fulfill the purpose God has for me and to please Him.

I'm grateful for realizing who I am in God. My confidence, beauty, and identity are all in Him. My life is truly divine. God called me from my mother's womb. I don't regret what I've been through because it was necessary. I am His and He is mine. There's nothing like unconditional love and intimacy with Jesus. Nothing can compare. I am loved. I am a daughter of the King, the Most High God. I am happy. I am resilient. I am capable. I am strong. I am beautiful. I am His masterpiece and so are you.

His Masterpiece

CONCLUSION

I AM ROYALTY

"My suffering was good for me, for it taught me to pay attention to your decrees" (Psalm 119:71)

The day Bishop Lockett christened me, who knew what I had to go through to get to a place of greatness? Who knew that a bright-eyed church girl would have to face addiction and abuse in order for her purpose to be fulfilled? Who knew my life would help other women? Everything I've faced is for the glory of God. I remember how I would be ashamed to talk about what I went through, but now, I can freely talk about it.

As you can see, I struggled to fit in, and I wanted so much for people to accept me. A lot of people are walking around trying to fill a void only Jesus can fill. Only God can show you who you are and what your purpose is on this earth. Your identity is in Him. You can try to drown it out, drink it out, sex it out, and club it out, but God is still there waiting for you to surrender to Him

If you have ever been taken advantage of, God can heal you in that area of your life. Allow Him to do so. Forgive the people who have wronged you and forgive yourself. Jesus died for that. He was also abused and taken advantage of; yet, He cried out, "Father, forgive them for they don't know what they are doing." You are here for such a time as this. You matter. If you don't know Jesus as your personal Lord and Savior, I invite you to say this prayer of salvation with me:

> *"Dear Jesus, I thank You for dying for me. I thank You for Your unconditional love to me. I am a sinner. I repent of all of my sins. Cleanse me. Purify me. Help me to forgive the people who have hurt me. Help me to forgive myself. Lord, I am Your vessel. Use me, God. I thank You that I am forgiven, and I am saved. In Jesus' name. Amen."*

Now, you're saved! Heaven is rejoicing! Your name is in the book of life! I encourage you to join a church of local believers, so you can grow in your identity in Christ. Be driven by your purpose and by eternity. Your testimony matters. Somebody's breakthrough is locked up in the testimony you're ashamed to tell. Jesus loves you, and He is there. Remember, you are fearfully and wonderfully made.

You are royalty. You are His masterpiece. I love you dearly.

In His love,

Kendra

National Domestic Violence Hotline
1-800-799-7233
www.thehotline.org